Don't Text That Man! Journal

RHONDA FINDLING

ISBN: 0615737064
ISBN-13: 978-0615737065

The front cover is a replication of the image of the
painting "Love" painted by Xhovalin Delia

INTRODUCTION

The Don't Text That Man! Journal is to help you express your feelings and thoughts about a man you are trying to let go of. You will find questions on each page with space for you to write. Good luck on your journey and remember – Don't Text That Man!

Today is day number _____ of
not contacting "that man"

- Did you have an urge to contact "that man" today?
  If you did write about it here.

- What do you think triggered your urge to
  contact "that man"?

- What action did you take to stop yourself from contacting "that man"?

- What did you tell yourself to not contact "that man"?

- How will you reward yourself for not contacting "that man" today?

Today is day number _____ of
not contacting "that man"

- Did you have an urge to contact "that man" today? If you did write about it here.

- What do you think triggered your urge to contact "that man"?

- What action did you take to stop yourself from contacting "that man"?

- What did you tell yourself to not contact "that man"?

- How will you reward yourself for not contacting "that man" today?

Today is day number _____ of
not contacting "that man"

- Did you have an urge to contact "that man" today? If you did write about it here.

- What do you think triggered your urge to contact "that man"?

- What action did you take to stop yourself from contacting "that man"?

- What did you tell yourself to not contact "that man"?

- How will you reward yourself for not contacting "that man" today?

Today is day number _____ of
not contacting "that man"

- Did you have an urge to contact "that man" today?
  If you did write about it here.

- What do you think triggered your urge to
  contact "that man"?

- What action did you take to stop yourself from contacting "that man"?

- What did you tell yourself to not contact "that man"?

- How will you reward yourself for not contacting "that man" today?

Today is day number _____ of
not contacting "that man"

- Did you have an urge to contact "that man" today? If you did write about it here.

- What do you think triggered your urge to contact "that man"?

- What action did you take to stop yourself from contacting "that man"?

- What did you tell yourself to not contact "that man"?

- How will you reward yourself for not contacting "that man" today?

Today is day number _____ of
not contacting "that man"

- Did you have an urge to contact "that man" today? If you did write about it here.

- What do you think triggered your urge to contact "that man"?

- What action did you take to stop yourself from contacting "that man"?

- What did you tell yourself to not contact "that man"?

- How will you reward yourself for not contacting "that man" today?

.

Today is day number _____ of
not contacting "that man"

- Did you have an urge to contact "that man" today?
  If you did write about it here.

- What do you think triggered your urge to
  contact "that man"?

- What action did you take to stop yourself from contacting "that man"?

- What did you tell yourself to not contact "that man"?

- How will you reward yourself for not contacting "that man" today?

Today is day number _____ of
not contacting "that man"

- Did you have an urge to contact "that man" today? If you did write about it here.

- What do you think triggered your urge to contact "that man"?

- What action did you take to stop yourself from contacting "that man"?

- What did you tell yourself to not contact "that man"?

- How will you reward yourself for not contacting "that man" today?

Today is day number _____ of
not contacting "that man"

- Did you have an urge to contact "that man" today? If you did write about it here.

- What do you think triggered your urge to contact "that man"?

- What action did you take to stop yourself from contacting "that man"?

- What did you tell yourself to not contact "that man"?

- How will you reward yourself for not contacting "that man" today?

Today is day number _____ of
not contacting "that man"

- Did you have an urge to contact "that man" today? If you did write about it here.

- What do you think triggered your urge to contact "that man"?

- What action did you take to stop yourself from contacting "that man"?

- What did you tell yourself to not contact "that man"?

- How will you reward yourself for not contacting "that man" today?

Today is day number _____ of
not contacting "that man"

- Did you have an urge to contact "that man" today?
  If you did write about it here.

- What do you think triggered your urge to
  contact "that man"?

- What action did you take to stop yourself from contacting "that man"?

- What did you tell yourself to not contact "that man"?

- How will you reward yourself for not contacting "that man" today?

Today is day number _____ of
not contacting "that man"

- Did you have an urge to contact "that man" today?
  If you did write about it here.

- What do you think triggered your urge to
  contact "that man"?

- What action did you take to stop yourself from contacting "that man"?

- What did you tell yourself to not contact "that man"?

- How will you reward yourself for not contacting "that man" today?

Today is day number _____ of
not contacting "that man"

- Did you have an urge to contact "that man" today?
  If you did write about it here.

- What do you think triggered your urge to
  contact "that man"?

- What action did you take to stop yourself from contacting "that man"?

- What did you tell yourself to not contact "that man"?

- How will you reward yourself for not contacting "that man" today?

Today is day number _____ of
not contacting "that man"

- Did you have an urge to contact "that man" today?
  If you did write about it here.

- What do you think triggered your urge to
  contact "that man"?

- What action did you take to stop yourself from contacting "that man"?

- What did you tell yourself to not contact "that man"?

- How will you reward yourself for not contacting "that man" today?

Today is day number _____ of
not contacting "that man"

- Did you have an urge to contact "that man" today?
  If you did write about it here.

- What do you think triggered your urge to
  contact "that man"?

- What action did you take to stop yourself from contacting "that man"?

- What did you tell yourself to not contact "that man"?

- How will you reward yourself for not contacting "that man" today?

Today is day number _____ of
not contacting "that man"

- Did you have an urge to contact "that man" today?
  If you did write about it here.

- What do you think triggered your urge to
  contact "that man"?

- What action did you take to stop yourself from contacting "that man"?

- What did you tell yourself to not contact "that man"?

- How will you reward yourself for not contacting "that man" today?

Today is day number _____ of
not contacting "that man"

- Did you have an urge to contact "that man" today? If you did write about it here.

- What do you think triggered your urge to contact "that man"?

- What action did you take to stop yourself from contacting "that man"?

- What did you tell yourself to not contact "that man"?

- How will you reward yourself for not contacting "that man" today?

Today is day number _____ of
not contacting "that man"

- Did you have an urge to contact "that man" today?
  If you did write about it here.

- What do you think triggered your urge to
  contact "that man"?

- What action did you take to stop yourself from contacting "that man"?

- What did you tell yourself to not contact "that man"?

- How will you reward yourself for not contacting "that man" today?

Today is day number _____ of
not contacting "that man"

- Did you have an urge to contact "that man" today?
  If you did write about it here.

- What do you think triggered your urge to
  contact "that man"?

- What action did you take to stop yourself from contacting "that man"?

- What did you tell yourself to not contact "that man"?

- How will you reward yourself for not contacting "that man" today?

Today is day number _____ of
not contacting "that man"

- Did you have an urge to contact "that man" today?
  If you did write about it here.

- What do you think triggered your urge to
  contact "that man"?

- What action did you take to stop yourself from contacting "that man"?

- What did you tell yourself to not contact "that man"?

- How will you reward yourself for not contacting "that man" today?

Today is day number _____ of
not contacting "that man"

- Did you have an urge to contact "that man" today?
  If you did write about it here.

- What do you think triggered your urge to
  contact "that man"?

- What action did you take to stop yourself from contacting "that man"?

- What did you tell yourself to not contact "that man"?

- How will you reward yourself for not contacting "that man" today?

Today is day number _____ of
not contacting "that man"

- Did you have an urge to contact "that man" today?
  If you did write about it here.

- What do you think triggered your urge to
  contact "that man"?

- What action did you take to stop yourself from contacting "that man"?

- What did you tell yourself to not contact "that man"?

- How will you reward yourself for not contacting "that man" today?

Today is day number _____ of
not contacting "that man"

- Did you have an urge to contact "that man" today?
  If you did write about it here.

- What do you think triggered your urge to
  contact "that man"?

- What action did you take to stop yourself from contacting "that man"?

- What did you tell yourself to not contact "that man"?

- How will you reward yourself for not contacting "that man" today?

Today is day number _____ of
not contacting "that man"

- Did you have an urge to contact "that man" today?
  If you did write about it here.

- What do you think triggered your urge to
  contact "that man"?

- What action did you take to stop yourself from contacting "that man"?

- What did you tell yourself to not contact "that man"?

- How will you reward yourself for not contacting "that man" today?

Today is day number _____ of
not contacting "that man"

- Did you have an urge to contact "that man" today?
  If you did write about it here.

- What do you think triggered your urge to
  contact "that man"?

- What action did you take to stop yourself from contacting "that man"?

- What did you tell yourself to not contact "that man"?

- How will you reward yourself for not contacting "that man" today?

Today is day number _____ of
not contacting "that man"

- Did you have an urge to contact "that man" today?
  If you did write about it here.

- What do you think triggered your urge to
  contact "that man"?

- What action did you take to stop yourself from contacting "that man"?

- What did you tell yourself to not contact "that man"?

- How will you reward yourself for not contacting "that man" today?

.

Today is day number _____ of
not contacting "that man"

- Did you have an urge to contact "that man" today?
  If you did write about it here.

- What do you think triggered your urge to
  contact "that man"?

- What action did you take to stop yourself from contacting "that man"?

- What did you tell yourself to not contact "that man"?

- How will you reward yourself for not contacting "that man" today?

Today is day number _____ of
not contacting "that man"

- Did you have an urge to contact "that man" today?
  If you did write about it here.

- What do you think triggered your urge to
  contact "that man"?

- What action did you take to stop yourself from contacting "that man"?

- What did you tell yourself to not contact "that man"?

- How will you reward yourself for not contacting "that man" today?

Today is day number _____ of
not contacting "that man"

- Did you have an urge to contact "that man" today?
  If you did write about it here.

.

- What do you think triggered your urge to
  contact "that man"?

- What action did you take to stop yourself from contacting "that man"?

- What did you tell yourself to not contact "that man"?

- How will you reward yourself for not contacting "that man" today?

Today is day number _____ of
not contacting "that man"

- Did you have an urge to contact "that man" today? If you did write about it here.

- What do you think triggered your urge to contact "that man"?

- What action did you take to stop yourself from contacting "that man"?

- What did you tell yourself to not contact "that man"?

- How will you reward yourself for not contacting "that man" today?

Today is day number _____ of
not contacting "that man"

- Did you have an urge to contact "that man" today? If you did write about it here.

- What do you think triggered your urge to contact "that man"?

- What action did you take to stop yourself from contacting "that man"?

- What did you tell yourself to not contact "that man"?

- How will you reward yourself for not contacting "that man" today?

Today is day number _____ of
not contacting "that man"

- Did you have an urge to contact "that man" today? If you did write about it here.

- What do you think triggered your urge to contact "that man"?

- What action did you take to stop yourself from contacting "that man"?

- What did you tell yourself to not contact "that man"?

- How will you reward yourself for not contacting "that man" today?

Today is day number _____ of
not contacting "that man"

- Did you have an urge to contact "that man" today?
  If you did write about it here.

- What do you think triggered your urge to
  contact "that man"?

- What action did you take to stop yourself from contacting "that man"?

- What did you tell yourself to not contact "that man"?

- How will you reward yourself for not contacting "that man" today?

Today is day number _____ of
not contacting "that man"

- Did you have an urge to contact "that man" today?
  If you did write about it here.

- What do you think triggered your urge to
  contact "that man"?

- What action did you take to stop yourself from contacting "that man"?

- What did you tell yourself to not contact "that man"?

- How will you reward yourself for not contacting "that man" today?

Today is day number _____ of
not contacting "that man"

- Did you have an urge to contact "that man" today?
  If you did write about it here.

- What do you think triggered your urge to
  contact "that man"?

- What action did you take to stop yourself from contacting "that man"?

- What did you tell yourself to not contact "that man"?

- How will you reward yourself for not contacting "that man" today?

Today is day number _____ of
not contacting "that man"

- Did you have an urge to contact "that man" today?
  If you did write about it here.

- What do you think triggered your urge to
  contact "that man"?

- What action did you take to stop yourself from contacting "that man"?

- What did you tell yourself to not contact "that man"?

- How will you reward yourself for not contacting "that man" today?

Today is day number _____ of
not contacting "that man"

- Did you have an urge to contact "that man" today?
  If you did write about it here.

- What do you think triggered your urge to
  contact "that man"?

- What action did you take to stop yourself from contacting "that man"?

- What did you tell yourself to not contact "that man"?

- How will you reward yourself for not contacting "that man" today?

Today is day number _____ of
not contacting "that man"

- Did you have an urge to contact "that man" today?
  If you did write about it here.

- What do you think triggered your urge to
  contact "that man"?

- What action did you take to stop yourself from contacting "that man"?

- What did you tell yourself to not contact "that man"?

- How will you reward yourself for not contacting "that man" today?

Today is day number _____ of
not contacting "that man"

- Did you have an urge to contact "that man" today?
  If you did write about it here.

- What do you think triggered your urge to
  contact "that man"?

- What action did you take to stop yourself from contacting "that man"?

- What did you tell yourself to not contact "that man"?

- How will you reward yourself for not contacting "that man" today?

Today is day number _____ of
not contacting "that man"

- Did you have an urge to contact "that man" today?
  If you did write about it here.

- What do you think triggered your urge to
  contact "that man"?

- What action did you take to stop yourself from contacting "that man"?

- What did you tell yourself to not contact "that man"?

- How will you reward yourself for not contacting "that man" today?

Today is day number _____ of
not contacting "that man"

- Did you have an urge to contact "that man" today?
  If you did write about it here.

- What do you think triggered your urge to
  contact "that man"?

- What action did you take to stop yourself from contacting "that man"?

- What did you tell yourself to not contact "that man"?

- How will you reward yourself for not contacting "that man" today?

Today is day number _____ of
not contacting "that man"

- Did you have an urge to contact "that man" today?
  If you did write about it here.

- What do you think triggered your urge to
  contact "that man"?

- What action did you take to stop yourself from contacting "that man"?

- What did you tell yourself to not contact "that man"?

- How will you reward yourself for not contacting "that man" today?

Today is day number _____ of
not contacting "that man"

- Did you have an urge to contact "that man" today? If you did write about it here.

- What do you think triggered your urge to contact "that man"?

- What action did you take to stop yourself from contacting "that man"?

- What did you tell yourself to not contact "that man"?

- How will you reward yourself for not contacting "that man" today?

Today is day number _____ of
not contacting "that man"

- Did you have an urge to contact "that man" today?
  If you did write about it here.

- What do you think triggered your urge to
  contact "that man"?

- What action did you take to stop yourself from contacting "that man"?

- What did you tell yourself to not contact "that man"?

- How will you reward yourself for not contacting "that man" today?

Today is day number _____ of
not contacting "that man"

- Did you have an urge to contact "that man" today?
  If you did write about it here.

- What do you think triggered your urge to
  contact "that man"?

- What action did you take to stop yourself from contacting "that man"?

- What did you tell yourself to not contact "that man"?

- How will you reward yourself for not contacting "that man" today?

Today is day number _____ of not contacting "that man"

- Did you have an urge to contact "that man" today? If you did write about it here.

- What do you think triggered your urge to contact "that man"?

- What action did you take to stop yourself from contacting "that man"?

- What did you tell yourself to not contact "that man"?

- How will you reward yourself for not contacting "that man" today?

.

Today is day number _____ of
not contacting "that man"

- Did you have an urge to contact "that man" today?
  If you did write about it here.

- What do you think triggered your urge to
  contact "that man"?

- What action did you take to stop yourself from contacting "that man"?

- What did you tell yourself to not contact "that man"?

- How will you reward yourself for not contacting "that man" today?

Today is day number _____ of
not contacting "that man"

- Did you have an urge to contact "that man" today?
  If you did write about it here.

- What do you think triggered your urge to
  contact "that man"?

- What action did you take to stop yourself from contacting "that man"?

- What did you tell yourself to not contact "that man"?

- How will you reward yourself for not contacting "that man" today?

Today is day number _____ of
not contacting "that man"

- Did you have an urge to contact "that man" today? If you did write about it here.

- What do you think triggered your urge to contact "that man"?

- What action did you take to stop yourself from contacting "that man"?

- What did you tell yourself to not contact "that man"?

- How will you reward yourself for not contacting "that man" today?

Today is day number _____ of
not contacting "that man"

- Did you have an urge to contact "that man" today? If you did write about it here.

- What do you think triggered your urge to contact "that man"?

- What action did you take to stop yourself from contacting "that man"?

- What did you tell yourself to not contact "that man"?

- How will you reward yourself for not contacting "that man" today?

Today is day number _____ of
not contacting "that man"

- Did you have an urge to contact "that man" today?
  If you did write about it here.

- What do you think triggered your urge to
  contact "that man"?

- What action did you take to stop yourself from contacting "that man"?

- What did you tell yourself to not contact "that man"?

- How will you reward yourself for not contacting "that man" today?

Today is day number _____ of
not contacting "that man"

- Did you have an urge to contact "that man" today? If you did write about it here.

- What do you think triggered your urge to contact "that man"?

- What action did you take to stop yourself from contacting "that man"?

- What did you tell yourself to not contact "that man"?

- How will you reward yourself for not contacting "that man" today?

Today is day number _____ of
not contacting "that man"

- Did you have an urge to contact "that man" today?
  If you did write about it here.

- What do you think triggered your urge to
  contact "that man"?

- What action did you take to stop yourself from contacting "that man"?

- What did you tell yourself to not contact "that man"?

- How will you reward yourself for not contacting "that man" today?

Today is day number _____ of
not contacting "that man"

- Did you have an urge to contact "that man" today?
  If you did write about it here.

- What do you think triggered your urge to
  contact "that man"?

- What action did you take to stop yourself from contacting "that man"?

- What did you tell yourself to not contact "that man"?

- How will you reward yourself for not contacting "that man" today?

Today is day number _____ of
not contacting "that man"

- Did you have an urge to contact "that man" today?
  If you did write about it here.

- What do you think triggered your urge to
  contact "that man"?

- What action did you take to stop yourself from contacting "that man"?

- What did you tell yourself to not contact "that man"?

- How will you reward yourself for not contacting "that man" today?

Today is day number _____ of
not contacting "that man"

- Did you have an urge to contact "that man" today?
  If you did write about it here.

- What do you think triggered your urge to
  contact "that man"?

- What action did you take to stop yourself from contacting "that man"?

- What did you tell yourself to not contact "that man"?

- How will you reward yourself for not contacting "that man" today?

.

Today is day number _____ of
not contacting "that man"

- Did you have an urge to contact "that man" today?
  If you did write about it here.

- What do you think triggered your urge to
  contact "that man"?

- What action did you take to stop yourself from contacting "that man"?

- What did you tell yourself to not contact "that man"?

- How will you reward yourself for not contacting "that man" today?

Today is day number _____ of
not contacting "that man"

- Did you have an urge to contact "that man" today?
  If you did write about it here.

- What do you think triggered your urge to
  contact "that man"?

- What action did you take to stop yourself from contacting "that man"?

- What did you tell yourself to not contact "that man"?

- How will you reward yourself for not contacting "that man" today?

Today is day number _____ of
not contacting "that man"

- Did you have an urge to contact "that man" today?
  If you did write about it here.

- What do you think triggered your urge to
  contact "that man"?

- What action did you take to stop yourself from contacting "that man"?

- What did you tell yourself to not contact "that man"?

- How will you reward yourself for not contacting "that man" today?

Today is day number _____ of
not contacting "that man"

- Did you have an urge to contact "that man" today?
  If you did write about it here.

- What do you think triggered your urge to
  contact "that man"?

- What action did you take to stop yourself from contacting "that man"?

- What did you tell yourself to not contact "that man"?

- How will you reward yourself for not contacting "that man" today?

Today is day number _____ of
not contacting "that man"

- Did you have an urge to contact "that man" today?
  If you did write about it here.

- What do you think triggered your urge to
  contact "that man"?

- What action did you take to stop yourself from contacting "that man"?

- What did you tell yourself to not contact "that man"?

- How will you reward yourself for not contacting "that man" today?

Today is day number _____ of
not contacting "that man"

- Did you have an urge to contact "that man" today? If you did write about it here.

- What do you think triggered your urge to contact "that man"?

- What action did you take to stop yourself from contacting "that man"?

- What did you tell yourself to not contact "that man"?

- How will you reward yourself for not contacting "that man" today?

Today is day number _____ of
not contacting "that man"

- Did you have an urge to contact "that man" today? If you did write about it here.

- What do you think triggered your urge to contact "that man"?

- What action did you take to stop yourself from contacting "that man"?

- What did you tell yourself to not contact "that man"?

- How will you reward yourself for not contacting "that man" today?

Today is day number _____ of
not contacting "that man"

- Did you have an urge to contact "that man" today?
  If you did write about it here.

- What do you think triggered your urge to
  contact "that man"?

- What action did you take to stop yourself from contacting "that man"?

- What did you tell yourself to not contact "that man"?

- How will you reward yourself for not contacting "that man" today?

Today is day number _____ of
not contacting "that man"

- Did you have an urge to contact "that man" today?
  If you did write about it here.

- What do you think triggered your urge to
  contact "that man"?

- What action did you take to stop yourself from contacting "that man"?

- What did you tell yourself to not contact "that man"?

- How will you reward yourself for not contacting "that man" today?

Today is day number _____ of
not contacting "that man"

- Did you have an urge to contact "that man" today? If you did write about it here.

- What do you think triggered your urge to contact "that man"?

- What action did you take to stop yourself from contacting "that man"?

- What did you tell yourself to not contact "that man"?

- How will you reward yourself for not contacting "that man" today?

Today is day number _____ of
not contacting "that man"

- Did you have an urge to contact "that man" today?
  If you did write about it here.

- What do you think triggered your urge to
  contact "that man"?

- What action did you take to stop yourself from contacting "that man"?

- What did you tell yourself to not contact "that man"?

- How will you reward yourself for not contacting "that man" today?

Today is day number _____ of
not contacting "that man"

- Did you have an urge to contact "that man" today?
  If you did write about it here.

- What do you think triggered your urge to
  contact "that man"?

- What action did you take to stop yourself from contacting "that man"?

- What did you tell yourself to not contact "that man"?

- How will you reward yourself for not contacting "that man" today?

Today is day number _____ of
not contacting "that man"

- Did you have an urge to contact "that man" today? If you did write about it here.

- What do you think triggered your urge to contact "that man"?

- What action did you take to stop yourself from contacting "that man"?

- What did you tell yourself to not contact "that man"?

- How will you reward yourself for not contacting "that man" today?

Today is day number _____ of
not contacting "that man"

- Did you have an urge to contact "that man" today?
  If you did write about it here.

- What do you think triggered your urge to
  contact "that man"?

- What action did you take to stop yourself from contacting "that man"?

- What did you tell yourself to not contact "that man"?

- How will you reward yourself for not contacting "that man" today?

Today is day number _____ of
not contacting "that man"

- Did you have an urge to contact "that man" today?
  If you did write about it here.

- What do you think triggered your urge to
  contact "that man"?

- What action did you take to stop yourself from contacting "that man"?

- What did you tell yourself to not contact "that man"?

- How will you reward yourself for not contacting "that man" today?

Today is day number _____ of
not contacting "that man"

- Did you have an urge to contact "that man" today? If you did write about it here.

- What do you think triggered your urge to contact "that man"?

- What action did you take to stop yourself from contacting "that man"?

- What did you tell yourself to not contact "that man"?

- How will you reward yourself for not contacting "that man" today?

Today is day number _____ of not contacting "that man"

- Did you have an urge to contact "that man" today? If you did write about it here.

- What do you think triggered your urge to contact "that man"?

- What action did you take to stop yourself from contacting "that man"?

- What did you tell yourself to not contact "that man"?

- How will you reward yourself for not contacting "that man" today?

Today is day number _____ of
not contacting "that man"

- Did you have an urge to contact "that man" today?
  If you did write about it here.

- What do you think triggered your urge to
  contact "that man"?

- What action did you take to stop yourself from contacting "that man"?

- What did you tell yourself to not contact "that man"?

- How will you reward yourself for not contacting "that man" today?

Today is day number _____ of
not contacting "that man"

- Did you have an urge to contact "that man" today?
  If you did write about it here.

- What do you think triggered your urge to
  contact "that man"?

- What action did you take to stop yourself from contacting "that man"?

- What did you tell yourself to not contact "that man"?

- How will you reward yourself for not contacting "that man" today?

Today is day number _____ of
not contacting "that man"

- Did you have an urge to contact "that man" today?
  If you did write about it here.

- What do you think triggered your urge to
  contact "that man"?

- What action did you take to stop yourself from contacting "that man"?

- What did you tell yourself to not contact "that man"?

- How will you reward yourself for not contacting "that man" today?

.

Today is day number _____ of
not contacting "that man"

- Did you have an urge to contact "that man" today? If you did write about it here.

- What do you think triggered your urge to contact "that man"?

- What action did you take to stop yourself from contacting "that man"?

- What did you tell yourself to not contact "that man"?

- How will you reward yourself for not contacting "that man" today?

Today is day number _____ of
not contacting "that man"

- Did you have an urge to contact "that man" today?
  If you did write about it here.

- What do you think triggered your urge to
  contact "that man"?

- What action did you take to stop yourself from contacting "that man"?

- What did you tell yourself to not contact "that man"?

- How will you reward yourself for not contacting "that man" today?

Today is day number _____ of
not contacting "that man"

- Did you have an urge to contact "that man" today? If you did write about it here.

- What do you think triggered your urge to contact "that man"?

- What action did you take to stop yourself from contacting "that man"?

- What did you tell yourself to not contact "that man"?

- How will you reward yourself for not contacting "that man" today?

Today is day number _____ of
not contacting "that man"

- Did you have an urge to contact "that man" today?
  If you did write about it here.

- What do you think triggered your urge to
  contact "that man"?

- What action did you take to stop yourself from contacting "that man"?

- What did you tell yourself to not contact "that man"?

- How will you reward yourself for not contacting "that man" today?

Today is day number _____ of
not contacting "that man"

- Did you have an urge to contact "that man" today?
  If you did write about it here.

- What do you think triggered your urge to
  contact "that man"?

- What action did you take to stop yourself from contacting "that man"?

- What did you tell yourself to not contact "that man"?

- How will you reward yourself for not contacting "that man" today?

Today is day number _____ of
not contacting "that man"

- Did you have an urge to contact "that man" today? If you did write about it here.

- What do you think triggered your urge to contact "that man"?

- What action did you take to stop yourself from contacting "that man"?

- What did you tell yourself to not contact "that man"?

- How will you reward yourself for not contacting "that man" today?

Today is day number _____ of
not contacting "that man"

- Did you have an urge to contact "that man" today? If you did write about it here.

- What do you think triggered your urge to contact "that man"?

- What action did you take to stop yourself from contacting "that man"?

- What did you tell yourself to not contact "that man"?

- How will you reward yourself for not contacting "that man" today?

Today is day number _____ of
not contacting "that man"

- Did you have an urge to contact "that man" today?
  If you did write about it here.

- What do you think triggered your urge to
  contact "that man"?

- What action did you take to stop yourself from contacting "that man"?

- What did you tell yourself to not contact "that man"?

- How will you reward yourself for not contacting "that man" today?

Today is day number _____ of
not contacting "that man"

- Did you have an urge to contact "that man" today? If you did write about it here.

- What do you think triggered your urge to contact "that man"?

- What action did you take to stop yourself from contacting "that man"?

- What did you tell yourself to not contact "that man"?

- How will you reward yourself for not contacting "that man" today?

Today is day number _____ of
not contacting "that man"

- Did you have an urge to contact "that man" today? If you did write about it here.

- What do you think triggered your urge to contact "that man"?

- What action did you take to stop yourself from contacting "that man"?

- What did you tell yourself to not contact "that man"?

- How will you reward yourself for not contacting "that man" today?

Today is day number _____ of
not contacting "that man"

- Did you have an urge to contact "that man" today?
  If you did write about it here.

- What do you think triggered your urge to
  contact "that man"?

- What action did you take to stop yourself from contacting "that man"?

- What did you tell yourself to not contact "that man"?

- How will you reward yourself for not contacting "that man" today?

Today is day number _____ of
not contacting "that man"

- Did you have an urge to contact "that man" today?
  If you did write about it here.

- What do you think triggered your urge to
  contact "that man"?

- What action did you take to stop yourself from contacting "that man"?

- What did you tell yourself to not contact "that man"?

- How will you reward yourself for not contacting "that man" today?

Today is day number _____ of
not contacting "that man"

- Did you have an urge to contact "that man" today? If you did write about it here.

- What do you think triggered your urge to contact "that man"?

- What action did you take to stop yourself from contacting "that man"?

- What did you tell yourself to not contact "that man"?

- How will you reward yourself for not contacting "that man" today?

Today is day number _____ of not contacting "that man"

- Did you have an urge to contact "that man" today? If you did write about it here.

- What do you think triggered your urge to contact "that man"?

- What action did you take to stop yourself from contacting "that man"?

- What did you tell yourself to not contact "that man"?

- How will you reward yourself for not contacting "that man" today?

Made in the USA
San Bernardino, CA
20 March 2018